Visitors are Welcomed with Efficiency

West Point addresses its international fame and three million visitors each year with information-laden efficiency. At Pershing Center, located in the Village of Highland Falls, one finds both a Visitors Center and the West Point Museum, two important stops when touring the United States Military Academy.

Tickets for a professionally guided bus tour may be purchased at the USMA Visitors Center in Highland Falls, NY, just outside West Point's Thayer Gate. You should start your visit with a 30-minute orientation at the Visitors Center. A West Point cadet's daily schedule is shown through photographs and multi-media presentations, conveying the challenging life that prepares cadets for service to the nation as U.S. Army officers.

Just a short walk from the Visitors Center is the renowned West Point Museum. It contains world-class collections in modern galleries exploring four distinct story lines, beginning with *West Point through 200 Years*. The *History of the United States Army, American Wars* and *the History of Warfare* are also explored in detail. Additionally, visitors can follow the development of large and small weapons through a visit to the museum's lower floors.

Well-stocked gift shops in both buildings offer a broad range of souvenirs as well as mail-order catalogs. There are restroom areas conveniently located in both facilities. The Thayer Hotel lies just within Thayer Gate, West Point's main entrance.

Fortress West Point: The Army's Oldest Post

General George Washington's command, issued in late 1777, was clear.

"Seize the present opportunity and employ your whole force and all the means in your power for erecting and completing … such works and obstructions as may be necessary to defend and secure the river." Fortress West Point, spanning the Hudson Highlands, was the eventual result. The American flag has flown here since January 27, 1778, making it the oldest continually occupied post of the U.S. Army. However, defeat had preceded ultimate victory, as the patriots did not have an easy time fortifying and holding the Hudson Valley.

In 1775, New York's Provincial Congress cautioned the Continental Congress that was convened in Philadelphia. The New Yorkers warned that British mastery of the Hudson River "… will give them the entire command of the water communication with the Indian nations, effectually prevent all intercourse between the eastern and southern Confederates, divide our strength and enfeeble every effort for our common preservation and security."

The Philadelphia delegates agreed. The lower Hudson River's broad expanses offered no stronghold sites. The 16-mile stretch through the Hudson Highlands above Peekskill provided the best opportunity for a defensive position. Without military expertise to call on, progress was slow. After a year of indecisiveness, inadequate fortifications, designed by inexperienced engineers and undermanned by militia, were in place along the Hudson. The militia proved no match for the British regulars in October of 1777. Tory betrayal of approach routes to river-covering Forts Montgomery

Captured British cannon from the 1777 victory at Saratoga and 13 links from the Hudson-blocking Great Chain displayed at Trophy Point help explain America's Revolutionary war success.

and Clinton at the southern approach to the Highlands led to a 30-minute battle and an American defeat. A minor fort on Constitution Island, opposite West Point, was quickly taken as well.

The Redcoat force of 2,500 men under Sir Henry Clinton got back in their boats and sailed north on the river he called "the Key of America." The Redcoats burned the state capital at Kingston and expected to join forces with General John Burgoyne in his coordinated thrust from Canada when news of another defeat on the Hudson River's banks was received. Now it was the British turn to weep.

Patriot Generals Horatio Gates and Benedict Arnold, leading 20,000 Continental Line and militia, captured 5,000 British regulars at the pivotal battle of Saratoga. The tides of war had turned on the tidal river that flowed two ways. A surge of Bluecoats was headed Clinton's way. Sir Henry sailed south to

New York City. General Washington now controlled the Hudson from the Highlands north.

British guns captured at Saratoga were soon manned by American artillerymen at West Point. The French, impressed by the Saratoga victory, cast their lot with the Americans. Shiploads of troops and arms came to Washington's support. After all, they had a common enemy – the British.

During the spring of 1778, Washington enlisted European expertise to capitalize on that "present opportunity" that followed Burgoyne's surrender. The engineering competency of Polish Colonel Tadeusz Kosciuszko harnessed the patriots' picks and shovels. While they were building a fortified ring of fire to plug the narrow cleft in the Highlands' granite, the Americans set about blocking its waters as well. A giant wooden boom spanned the Hudson River between Constitution Island and West Point. That barrier was designed to slow British warships from their intent to ram its upstream neighbor, a log-floated 500-foot long chain whose 120-pound links had been forged by local blacksmiths at the Sterling Ironworks – ahead of schedule and under budget!

Present-day West Point cadets learn the timeless need to control terrain as they hike up to Fort Putnam and Redoubt Four. The cadets are taking a *staff ride*, an analytical tour of a historic battlefield. Each cadet is challenged to become a role-playing subject expert about Fortress West Point during the American Revolution. When the military history teacher conducting the four-hour class turns to a cadet and asks, "Colonel Kosciuszko, what was your plan? And, why was it better than the giant fortress plan offered by your French predecessor, Colonel de la Radiere?", the instructor is facilitating learning, not offering instruction.

Kosciuszko-for-a-day makes it clear how "his" plan created a fortified area with three concentric rings of mutually supportive strong points. He talks about forts that controlled the river and protected the chain, forts that protected the river-controlling forts from land-based attacks, redoubts which covered everything from the highest ground.

The colonel will point out 14 fortified positions training 100 cannons on every possible approach the British might take. And, his fellow cadets will grasp that Kosciuszko's ideas were "modern." Those plans depended on mobile militia forces that could be raised quickly and move swiftly along narrow mountain trails to reinforce a network of ridgetop strongholds. Put all your hopes on a gigantic French-style river edge castle and you have a real siege-relief problem.

Cadets role playing the American soldier are quick to respond with details of everyday life – as bad as Valley Forge – lots of pick and shovel work to build river-covering Fort Clinton's 600-foot long walls. They were 9-feet high and 20-feet thick. Redoubts protecting riverside fortifications from land attack averaged 6-feet high and 6-feet thick.

As Academy instructors use historic West Point for their classroom, challenging role-playing cadets to bring history alive, the *staff ride's* interactivity conveys a critical thought. "By its very nature, war is a highly complex affair with a virtually infinite number of variables. Conducted in a dynamic environment by human beings, themselves infinitely variable in personality and in war is played out on a three-dimensional chessboard of terrain.

West Point Museum. Extensive explanatory plaques cover the period 1776-1898. After the Mexican War (1845-48), captured cannon were sent to the U.S. Military Academy. Commanding General Winfield Scott said that because of West Point graduates, "...in less than two campaigns we conquered a great country and a peace without the loss of a single battle or skirmish." ...Later those young comrades-in-arms rose to become generals – opposing generals – in 55 of the 60 most important battles of our four-year Civil War. Some call it a "West Pointer's War."

The Plain at West Point is certainly the U.S. Army's most hallowed training terrain. In July of 1779, the Continental Line's imported taskmaster, Friedrich von Steuben, arduously drilled infantry here. These crack troops then followed General "Mad Anthony" Wayne in a midnight bayonet raid on nearby Stony Point, a fort they had just lost to the British. The cost to His Majesty's forces: the jumping off point for another campaign to take the Hudson Highlands, 600 "Lobsterbacks" and a good store of fine weapons. So much for the idea of another easy British campaign up-river. The British never challenged West Point by force again, though they attempted to take it by treachery.

General Benedict Arnold, the brave, but vain, hero of the Patriot victory at Saratoga, was dissatisfied with his slow promotion by the Continental Congress. He sought to better his lot by switching sides. Twenty thousand pounds sterling was Arnold's price for intentionally degrading West Point's defenses and delivering the plans for West Point to the British Adjutant Major John Andre. Andre's capture as a spy not only nipped the budding plot, it also sent Arnold scampering downstream to British-held New York City. His name is used in American history books as a synonym for traitor. General Washington immediately took over command, called up the militia and brought West Point to full battle stance. The British never attacked since the element of surprise had been lost.

In 1781, Washington's main force of Continentals was encamped north of Fortress West Point. They were prepared for a final showdown. A quick march into the South put surprise on their side. In alliance with French troops commanded by General Rochembeau, supported by shipboard artillery of the French Caribbean Fleet under Admiral de Grasse, Washington besieged Yorktown, Virginia.

The Patriots' Fife and Drum Corps played "The World Turned Upside Down" as Lord Cornwallis' army of 7,000 stacked arms in surrender. The War for Independence was won. Washington and his army returned to their safe haven in the Hudson Valley and waited two years for a peace treaty.

West Point's historic messages are not conveyed by angry cannons alone. On May 31, 1782, 500 illustrious citizens of the Hudson Valley invaded Fortress West Point by invitation of George Washington. The citizens of the new Democracy gathered within a gloriously decorated colonnade of freshly cut trees, ostensibly to celebrate the birth of the Dauphin, heir apparent to the ancient Monarchy of France. There was dining and dancing and celebratory music. Flowery toasts to independence and freedom were followed by endless firings of 13 cannons, which in turn signaled outlying troops to initiate a feu de joie. The relay chain of musket firing lit the night like a fiery wave, descending through the Eastern Highlands to Garrison, then back up-river to West Point.

Patriotic outpourings, begun in that long ago West Point moment, continue on in the series of free summer Sunday evening concerts at Trophy Point. The Hellcat Drum and Bugle Corps

Drums & Bugles of the Hellcats continue a musical tradition that began in 1778. Behind them is the old Ordnance Compound where the U.S. Army once stored its main ammo supply.

offers up Revolutionary War tunes as well as Sousa. When the USMA band closes its season on Labor Day weekend with Tchaikovsky's *1812 Overture*, the concert-ending cannons and fireworks bounce off the same flinty ramparts that resounded during that 1782 victory celebration. It is easy to drift back in time at West Point: listen hard and you may hear George Washington joining his guests in a still-echoing colonial hoo-rah. *Huzzah! Huzzah! Huzzah!*

CADET BARRACKS.

GENERAL VIEW OF WEST POINT.

ACADEMY.

ART'Y DEPOT.

THE PLAIN.

HOTEL.

SAPPER DEPOT.

RIDE HALL.

The Academy – Founded in 1802

As one graduating cadet observed, "A lot of this architecture, which they call Military gothic, reminds us that we are going into a very serious profession."

New cadets are issued *Bugle Notes*, a small book packed with West Point information that must be learned quickly and repeated almost word-for-word upon demand. For example there is a description of the Academy's architecture. *"The buildings of the Military Academy give an impression of massiveness and strength, their sturdy design bespeaks the inherent character of the Corps, the enduring spirit of the Long Gray Line. The granite-faced structures harmonize well with the winding river and rugged hills that form their background."*

At first, West Point's architectural design sweepstakes was a struggle between Gothic revival and Greek revival. The Goths won, battlements up! By 1857, West Point presented itself as a very well appointed Academy for 250 cadets. The campus emulated the Gothic buildings of Oxford University. The recent Historic Structures Inventory of USMA taken by the National Park Service noted that West Point's "distinct fortress-like appearance must be preserved."

That appearance has been well guarded. After West Point's Centennial in 1902, Congress recognized its importance to the nation with a $5.5 million construction appropriation. Improvements were needed to serve an expanded Corps of Cadets that numbered 1,300 on the eve of World War I. The program called for new Cadet Barracks, Academic and Administration Buildings, a Chapel and Riding Hall.

The Dean's House heads up "Professors Row." It is a classic Hudson River Valley Victorian villa, built in 1857.

The criteria by which architectural proposals were to be judged were clearly stated by the colonel/ professor in charge of the expansion. "It is of the highest importance to preserve intact the structural sentiment which gives character and individuality to the Academy," he stated. The Boston firm of Cram, Goodhue and Ferguson was chosen because their Gothic style attempted to "... harmonize with the majority of the existing buildings, and prolong rather than revolutionize the spirit of the place." Ensuing expansions have respected those Gothic granite designs. The present day buildings accommodate 4,000 cadets.

West Point's curriculum designer, Sylvanus Thayer, was from Braintree, Massachusetts. Thayer was a Dartmouth College graduate when he entered West Point. Graduating from the Academy in 1808, Thayer served with distinction in the War of 1812. He was chosen by the Secretary of War to make a tour of European military establishments and educational institutions. He returned with a thousand books for the West Point Library. Thayer also returned with a full understanding of

A granite jewel box, Pershing Barracks opened in 1895 as the West Academic Building.

the educational structure that was needed to assure America had a supply of home grown Kosciuszkos and Von Steubens.

When Thayer was appointed superintendent of West Point in 1817, he transformed a floundering institution into America's foremost scientific university. Fondly called "The Father of the Academy," Thayer instituted the Academic Board to nurture intellectual skills. The Commandant of Cadets' office was responsible for instructing cadets in military skills.

Thayer rejected the European system of large lectures followed by small discussion groups and insisted that all instruction be offered in small sections of 18 or less. This allowed the use of *The Thayer Method: "Every cadet recites in every subject every day."* The cadets were responsible for learning the material before class, not through listening in a lecture hall. Today's West Point faculty respects Thayer as a prophetic educator, pioneering the basic principle of modern active learning: "the student must be engaged with the subject matter."

West Point's claim to fame as America's first engineering school dates from the Thayer superintendency, 1817-1833. Colonel Thayer and his Professor of Engineering, Colonel Dennis Hart Mahan, saw their graduates excel in both military and civil engineering challenges put forth by an expanding nation. West Point graduates later went on to head the newly established engineering schools at Harvard, Yale, Dartmouth and Michigan.

The creation of the military academy, like victory in the American Revolution, did not come easily. Washington's last official letter was written on December 12, 1799. Responding to Alexander Hamilton's proposal for a national military academy, Washington affirmed that "The establishment of an institution of this kind, upon a respectable and extensive basis, has ever been considered by me as an object of primary importance to this country."

Though Washington was indebted to foreign military experts such as Kosciuszko and Von Steuben for Fortress West Point's survival, he strongly desired that such expertise could be nurtured on American soil. But the new republic was very cautious about replacing the Sirs and Lords it had overthrown with an American military aristocracy.

New cadets are issued computers before academic instruction begins. The campus network links them with their e-mail accounts, USMA instructors, academic resources, the worldwide web as well as other evolving challenges. New cadets moving into Central Barracks (above) in 1851 learned about the telegraph.

Ironically, Thomas Jefferson, a long-term opponent of the proposed military academy, had a change of heart when he became President. He signed legislation creating the United States Military Academy, West Point, New York, on March 16, 1802. The Academy was located at the site of the nation's ordnance depot and the headquarters of the Army's Corps of Engineers.

Historians now feel that Jefferson's support stemmed not from his interest in furthering the scientific education necessary for sound military engineering, but perhaps from his zest for politics. Academy appointments would provide higher education to sons of his non-aristocratic followers, democratizing the Army leadership. The move towards even-handed appointments was slow but sure. By 1826, Congressmen were each asked to nominate one cadet. In 1843, the academy administration squelched concerns that West Point was furthering an aristocracy by doing an economic survey of the cadets' parents. Only six were born to wealth, while 26 came from homes of "reduced means." The remaining 156 were middle class.

The quest for well-qualified, impartially examined candidates to lead our military has continued. Competitively awarded congressional appointments are the main route to education at the U.S. Military Academy, the U.S. Naval Academy (1845), the U.S. Coast Guard Academy (1873) and the U.S. Air Force Academy (1955). President George H.W. Bush described our national military academies as "meritocracy in action."

Peter Dawkins, Class of 1959, was Cadet First Captain, captain of the football team, a Heisman Trophy winner, a Rhodes scholar and a combat leader in Vietnam. Dawkins, now working in the financial community, has no reluctance in expressing the need for future leaders. "Many of us feel in our bones that the world is not going to get any less dangerous, and is not going to be any less in need of good leadership for the Army."

Brigadier General Fletcher Lamkin, Class of 1964 and former Dean of the Academic Board, spoke of West Point's response to the Army's leadership needs.

"We are constantly examining the question, 'What should the leaders of the 21st century army have as their intellectual underpinning?'" said General Lamkin. "Our faculty includes people who have served in Vietnam, Grenada, Desert Storm, Somalia, and Bosnia. They have warfighting and peacekeeping experience to share with the cadets they instruct and mentor. As officers it

Carved on the Academy's buildings one finds a recurring heraldic theme: the American eagle, the national shield, the West Point motto "Duty Honor, Country", and the helmet of Pallas Athena, the Greek warrior goddess.

The Thayer Method – small classes, well-versed instructors, and daily discussion of each subject - is at USMA's academic core.

our job to be prepared, to handle every thing those types of operations entail. The demands are for a combination – breadth of knowledge and depth of knowledge.

"A leader of soldiers is someone you would trust, someone who wouldn't do anything stupid with soldiers' lives. They have to understand good order and discipline, rules and regulations, and they learn to obey commands which are legal. These young officers will know how to think their way through a moral, ethical dilemma – a My Lai – and do the right thing. You are faced with complex issues when you're on the ground in a war. You are frustrated, you have been fighting. But we are critical thinkers, educated people, and not robots. It's an American ethic to challenge.

"The folks who emigrated to this country left oppressive governments, governments that didn't respect their rights. Good education increases our chances to do the right thing."

With twenty years of troop-leading experience, General Lamkin is aware that it takes a lot of knowledge, work and compassion to earn respect and assure effectiveness "out there." With thousands of U.S. Army soldiers deployed on operational or training missions in 90 countries, "out there" is next door. American military forces have deployed to crisis areas more than 30 times since the fall of the Berlin Wall. No wonder "from peacekeeping to warfighting" describes the modern army's challenges.

To enable its graduates to anticipate and respond effectively to a world of uncertainty, of continuing technological, social, political and economic change, West Point spelled out specific attributes it wanted to develop through its curriculum. Verbs headed each goal – think and act, understand, use, draw on, communicate, recognize and demonstrate.

As the 21st century began, the curriculum had 30 required core courses – 17 of them in Humanities and Social Sciences and 13 of them in Math, Science and Engineering. Where West Point once

The Demanding Daily Life of a Cadet –
Washington Hall's Cadet Mess seats the entire
Corps of Cadets, 4,000 strong, in six wings.
Cadet officers head each table. At the foot is
"The Gunner", a plebe who anxiously executes
precision pie cutting and dessert service.

Lifelong friendships are formed within the 32 companies. Cadets are housed two or three to a room on mixed gender floors. About 15% of the Corps are females; 20% are minorities.

emphasized engineering as befits the nation's pioneering engineering school, its 13 academic departments now offer 24 fields of study and 21 optional majors. Cadets leaving a class in *International Relations* can move on to the next hour's challenge, *Land Use Planning and Management*. Senior year capstone projects engage cadets in original research in their major fields. Eighty Military Academy graduates since 1923 have joined the ranks of Rhodes scholars.

Visitors to West Point take notice of the highly energetic pace of cadet life. Each weekday at noon cadets form up for their lunchtime march into Washington Hall. They have been on the go since Reveille at 6:30 a.m. and in class since 7:35 for a three-hour block of instruction. After lunch, there are more academic classes, athletics, drill and ceremonies and military and physical training. Intramural sports leagues thrive under coaching by senior cadets.

The evening study period begins at 7:30 p.m. and lasts through taps. All cadets must be in their rooms by 11:30 p.m. and lights are out at midnight. Back in 1914, someone at the Academy deter-

mined that there were more than 18,000 opportunities for a cadet to be late at some duty or drill during his course. Cadets have not been able to re-tabulate that figure since then, lest they be late themselves.

A Brigadier General serves as Commandant of Cadets at West Point and is in charge of the Academy's rigorous military and physical skills programs. Cadets have four full summer sessio

of military training, either at West Point's 16,000 acres of training grounds or with U.S. Army units. The Department of Military Instruction also offers classes throughout the academic year.

The cadet ranks are structured just as the U.S. Army is structured. Fourth class cadets (freshmen) are privates; the third class (sophomores) serve as corporals; the second class cadets (juniors) are sergeants and cadets from the first class (seniors) hold the officer positions. This progressive structure is designed to develop command skills.

Each of the 32 cadet companies competes in 26 intramural sports. Physical education courses and proficiency tests assure that the young lieutenants will be capable of leading the way in their units. Teamwork and leadership skills are directly mentored within each company by its own two-person U.S. Army tactical team, a commissioned officer and a noncommissioned officer. Class standing on graduation is not determined by academics alone. Military skills count for 30% and physical skills count for 15%.

The Noncommissioned Officer Corps who have helped train the young cadets look forward to offering them their first salute as commissioned officers. That first returned salute is gladly received, for it is traditionally accompanied by an Eisenhower silver dollar, a token of esteem for the NCOs with whom the lieutenants will serve the nation.

"Beast Barracks," the six-week Cadet Basic Training program for new cadets, ends with the 12-mile march from Lake Frederick to a warm "Welcome Back" by the Superintendent's House.

Religion at West Point

West Point's student population is drawn from all 50 states and all walks of life. They bring to the Academy a true spiritual cross section of America and find their religious practices supported by chaplains of their faith and sponsored by on-post families. Cadet religious programs receive strong financial and spiritual support from Alumni, parents and national denominations. Privately funded construction provided USMA with Catholic (1900) and Jewish Chapels (1984).

The landscape-dominating, 1,500-seat Cadet Chapel rising above Washington Hall serves the Protestant cadet community. Completed in 1910 from architectural designs by Cram, Goodhue and Ferguson, its walls are hewn from locally quarried granite. Stained glass windows, donated by and dedicated to graduating classes, present key biblical personalities. The Sunday afternoon concert series is presented on the world's largest church organ. It has 19,000 pipes and 312 ranks.

The Cadet Prayer

O God, our Father, Thou Searcher of Human hearts, help us to draw near to thee in sincerity and truth. May our religion be filled with gladness and may our worship of Thee be natural.

Strengthen and increase our admiration for honest dealing and clean thinking and suffer not our hatred of hypocrisy and pretense ever to diminish. Encourage us in our endeavor to choose the harder right instead of the easier wrong, and never be content with a half-truth when the whole can be won.

Help us to maintain the honor of the Corps untarnished and unsullied and to show forth in our lives the ideals of West Point in doing our duty to Thee and to our country.

All of which we ask in the name of the Great Friend and Master of all. Amen.

national touring shows open to public ticket sale. Ike Hall's ballrooms host a continuous series of Cadet Hops. Ring Weekend steps off the graduating class's final year.

Open to the Public – Ike Hall Activities

What do cadets do when they aren't studying, drilling and playing intramural sports? Quite a bit! They come to the Academy with a broad range of personal interests and track records as leaders in their high school extracurricular programs. Cadets find over 100 clubs to keep them occupied after scheduled daily activities or on weekends. There are clubs that further their enjoyment of ballroom dancing, chess, flying, short wave radio and white water canoeing. Sports clubs offer chances for competition in a number of athletic areas not covered by West Point's intercollegiate athletic teams. West Point's "club teams" in rugby, power lifting and water polo have come home with national and regional honors.

One of the most popular clubs is "Theater Arts." Eisenhower Hall's 4,400-seat auditorium is second to Radio City Music Hall in size and has a far richer season. Though Ike Hall is 50 miles north of Broadway, the very best of Broadway entertainment has shown up on its stage. Headliners like Billy Joel, Elton John, Bob Dylan and James Taylor have performed here. Touring companies of Cats, West Side Story, South Pacific, Camelot, Les Miserables, A Chorus Line, Annie, Evita, and Sunset Boulevard have utilized cadets as ushers and spotlight operators, backstage hands and avid theatergoers.

Hudson Valley residents join the cadets as subscribers to season tickets or individual performances. First class cadets celebrate their arrival at one hundred nights before graduation with a tradi-tionally outrageous spoof of the Academy's foibles. It is surprisingly called "The One Hundredth Night Show." The cavorting firsties provide everyone – cadets, faculty, parents and others – with sharp satire of the most sacred West Point topics. Visitors can find out how to purchase tickets or obtain a schedule of events by contacting the Eisenhower Hall Box Office at (845) 938-4159.

Eisenhower Hall also serves as a home for a variety of cadet social activities. West Pointers call their dances "Hops" and they keep things 'hopping' most weekends. There are small hops, with music by the USMA Band's Jazz Knights and the Cadet Hop Band. There are disc jockey hops and there are big formals. Each class has its own formal hop weekend. There is Plebe-Parent Weekend, the 500th Night (before graduation) Weekend, Graduation Weekend and most importantly, Ring Weekend. This occurs in late August each year, celebrating the presentation of the class ring or "fat boy" as it is affectionately called.

With training that sharpens their focus on studies and energizes the response to a challenging program, about 80 percent of each class entering West Point receives their rings, graduates and is commissioned as second lieutenants. That retention rate is better than many of the highly selective American colleges and universities. As one cadet observes, "By your firstie year (senior), you know what you need to do; you get the job done; and have some fun along the way.'"

honor of Dennis Michie. This storied cadet organized the Army football team and led them against their first opponent – Navy! He lost his life on San Juan Hill in 1898.

Cadet Athletics – "It Isn't Just Football"

Weekend visitors to West Point are treated to one of America's great sporting events during the fall football season. Army football fans are well advised to buy tickets early, fill your picnic hampers and arrive in the morning. You will be treated to the Corps of Cadets in review on The Plain, your favorite barbecue tailgate menu in the parking lot, a hard-fought football game and the glorious fall foliage of the Hudson River Valley.

West Point's memorable moments have included the glorious 1940's when Army won National Championships from 1944-46 under Coach Earl "Red" Blaik, and football fans watched Heisman Trophy winners Glenn Davis and Felix "Doc" Blanchard become one of the most feared backfield tandems in college football history.

A veteran sports writer, well aware of Army's important 100-year, 1000-game football record, speaks insightfully about post-game locker room moments. "These athletes hold themselves to a high level, both on and off the field. I've seen some of their greatest personal victories come after a defeat. There's no finger pointing; they support each other." This sportswriter was describing what Army football teams do after each encounter --win or lose. It is almost like an "After Action Review" of the U.S. Army. "What did we do right? What did we do wrong? What can we do to improve our effort the next time around?"

West Point visitors can purchase tickets by calling the Army Ticket Office at 1-800-ARMYTIX. The staff handles sales of football, hockey, basketball and lacrosse games.

"I need an officer for a secret and dangerous mission. I want a West Point football player"; a World War II summons. Players smack the plaque in a pre-game ritual that confirms Army's can-do spirit.

Sports at West Point are not limited to intercollegiate competition. While USMA Superintendent from 1919-1922, then Brigadier General Douglas MacArthur developed a complete all-season intramural program designed to instill teamwork skills throughout the Corps. The innovation remains strong even today. As company teams compete for Brigade championships in 15 sports, the program fulfills MacArthur's intention: "Upon the fields of friendly strife, are sown the seeds that, upon other fields, on other days, will bear the fruits of victory."

Teamwork, stamina and the sheer will to win are evident throughout the intramural program. This spirit is also quite evident on football weekends. The Corps of Cadets, known to the football eleven as "The Twelfth Man," stands throughout the entire game until the clock runs out.

Sing-A-Long, Cheer-A-Long

The ROCKET CHEER starts with a whistle, then goes *Boom! – AHHH – USMA Rah! Rah! – USMA Rah! Rah! – Hoo-rah! – Hoo-rah! Army! – Rah! – Team! Team! Team!*

One of the country's best-known football fight songs is On Brave Old Army Team.

The Army Team's the pride and dream of every heart in gray – The Army Line you'll ever find a terror in the fray; - And when the team is fighting for the Black and Gray and Gold – We're always near with song and cheer and this is the tale we're told: On Brave Old Army Team, on to the fray; Fight on to victory, for that's the fearless Army way.

When each game ends and dusk falls on Saturday afternoons at Michie Stadium, football players and the Corps of Cadets stand at attention and sing the Alma Mater in tribute to this renowned Academy.

Hail, Alma Mater dear, to us be ever near.
Help us thy motto bear through all the years.

Let duty be well performed, honor be e'er untarned.
Country be ever armed, West Point by thee.
Guide us, thy sons, aright, teach us by day, by night.
To keep thine honor bright, for thee to fight.
When we depart from thee, serving on land or sea,
May we still loyal be, West Point to thee.
And when our work is done, our course on earth is run,
May it be said, "Well done; be thou at peace."
E'er may that line of gray increase from day to day,
Live, serve, and die, we pray, West Point for thee.

is applied by the First Captain before the Army-Navy Game march-on. West Point professors attest to its importance during the chaos of battle.

"I Will Support and Defend"

The precision drill of the traditional Army-Navy Game march-on by the Corps of Cadets might delight the 18th century Prussian King Frederick the Great. But, as one West Point professor observed, Frederick "insisted common soldiers should fear their officers more than the enemy." West Pointers are not that kind of officer. Every cadet learns General John Schofield's *Definition of Discipline*, offered to the Corps in 1879.

"The discipline which makes the soldiers of a free country reliable in battle is not to be gained by harsh or tyrannical treatment. On the contrary, such treatment is far more likely to destroy than to make an army... He who feels the respect which is due to others cannot fail to inspire in them regard for himself." This high standard is part of the shared commitment West Point cadets make when they take the oath of allegiance on Graduation Day. *"I, _____, having been appointed an officer in the Army of the United States, indicated in the grade of Second Lieutenant, do solemnly swear that I will support and defend the Constitution of the United States against all enemies, foreign and domestic, that I will bear true faith and allegiance to the same, that I take this obligation freely, without any mental reservation or purpose of evasion; and that I will well and faithfully discharge the duties of the office which I am about to enter, so help me God.*

DUTY · HONOR · COUNTRY

VICTORY. THAT THE VERY OBSESSION OF YOUR PUBLIC SERVICE MUST BE
WIN. THE SURE KNOWLEDGE THAT IN WAR THERE IS NO SUBSTITUTE FOR
ACCOMPLISHMENT. YOURS IS THE PROFESSION OF ARMS — THE WILL TO
OUR WARS. ALL OTHER PUBLIC PURPOSES WILL FIND OTHERS FOR THEIR
YOUR MISSION REMAINS FIXED, DETERMINED, INVIOLABLE — IT IS TO WIN

The Thayer Addresses to the Corps

When General of the Army Douglas MacArthur delivered his "Duty, Honor, Country" speech to the Cadet Corps at his acceptance of the Sylvanus Thayer Award, he stirringly summarized a West Point graduate's responsibility. General MacArthur's challenges are carved in granite on benches surrounding his statue and committed to memory by incoming Plebes. Each year another leading citizen is recognized for past service to the nation and addresses the Corps of Cadets, expressing their own expectations and appreciation.

The late Congresswoman Barbara Jordan said, "I believe I am looking at an audience that includes future Thayer Award winners. By your desire to come to this place, by your admittance through a rigorous screening process and by your work while here, you have already shown that you are the resource from which leaders will emerge. If you do not develop honor, if you do not embrace the finest sense of justice that the human mind can frame, you will not be worthy of the confidence West Point and your country will place in you.

"Your mission statement should be a constant inspiration to you," Jordan continued. "Each graduate shall have the attributes essential to professional growth throughout a career as an officer of the regular Army," it reads in part, "Growth means change. Do not fear change. We have grown and excelled as a nation in no small part because of the work of your West Point family tree."

Bob Hope, whose holidays were spent entertaining American military all around the world, offered a series of laugh-grabbers during his Thayer Award acceptance speech.

"That review was magnificent," said Hope. "All those cadets moving in perfect unison, it restores my faith in life – it's nice to know there are still teenagers who can agree on something.

"This is a great institution. There's so much brass here, the saluting keeps the place air conditioned."

But not all of his lines were meant to draw laughter. He also offered appreciation. "For the last 25 years I've met and worked with the cream of our military, dedicated to keeping this country and its way of life firm and strong. I've laughed with them all over the world and I've never met a finer bunch. That's why this (Thayer Award) means so much to me."

Cadets move up through the ranks from 4th Class plebe to 1st Class firstie. Six-stripers head each 1,000-strong cadet regiment. Six stripes and a star – The First Captain. The cadet ranks emulate U.S. Army structure.

47 months of rigorous training sends white hats soaring. Graduation Week's parades, receptions and dances culminate in private bar pinnings as cadets become Army 2ⁿᵈ Lieutenants.

Graduating into Responsibility

"At West Point, our underlying principle is 'cooperate and graduate, rather than 'the survival of the fittest - may the best person win.' " That cadet insight was offered by Randall Lummer, USMA 2000.

"You are responsible for people other than yourself," he added. " 'I've got you covered' is a combat maneuver cry - and it applies to life within the cadet companies as well." Help from other cadets is there, consistently offered, ethically constrained.

Cadet mutual reliance is guided by the *Honor Code* under which they have lived. *A cadet will not lie, cheat, steal, or tolerate those who do* is a formal expression of an age-old warrior's creed.

When the First Captain says "Class Dismissed," cadets throw their hats into the air but they don't throw away personal responsibility for their own acts. Having just taken the oath which binds them for five years of service in the Army, they have assumed a broader mantle – responsibility for the lives of the soldiers whom they will lead. The Army which they enter – they go 'from gray to green' as their white hats descend – lives by another expression of military ethics, codified as *Army Values*. The words *Loyalty, Duty, Respect, Selfless Service, Honor, Integrity, Personal Courage* are as much a part of the modern American Soldier's life as the words *Duty, Honor, Country* are a part of cadet life.

Though West Point was once the exclusive source of officers for a smaller Army, America's increased world responsibilities have expanded schooling for leadership into Reserve Officer Training Corps programs at universities nationwide as well as Officer Candidate Schools within the Army. All U.S. Army officers can look forward to a continuing relationship with training and education. First stop is the Officer Basic Course within their branch: Infantry, Armor, Artillery, Aviation, Engineers, Finance, Military Intelligence, Air Defense Artillery, Chemical Corps, Adjutant General Corps, Military Police, Signal Corps, Transportation, Quartermaster. Once in the Army, their initial responsibility as platoon leading Lieutenants will be to see that their troops are well trained. As they rise in the ranks, they do so with additional education: Masters and Doctorates in their disciplines, as well as attendance at Advanced Officer Course, Combined Arms Services Staff School, Command & General Staff College and The War College. School is never out.

begin their reunions by honoring Sylvanus Thayer at his statue in front of the Superintendent's House (1820). Colonel Thayer was superintendent from 1817-1833.

"We All Take the Same Oath"

Returning "Old Grads" are special visitors during Graduation Week. Cadets confess to feeling tears on their cheeks as those who have 'been there and done that' pass between their honor cordon on the way to laying a wreath at Sylvanus Thayer's Statue. Thayer was not only the *Father of the Academy* but also was the first president of the Association of Graduates. The 'AOG' was founded in 1869 to "assist in the nation's healing process after the Civil War." Since a West Point general won 59 of the Civil War's 60 major battles, there was significant social and fraternal work to be done. Current Association of Graduate members have strong links, forged through student days and military service.

Let Bob Nulsen, Class of 1949, give you a sense of what it is like to be inside the Long Gray Line.

"Lived at West Point from the time I was 4 until I was 8," recalls Nulsen. "My father, a grad, was assigned as a tactical officer, responsible for one of the cadet battalions. Those parades stirred my soul a bit. Hiding behind the crowd, I tried to march along with them.

"As a cadet I quickly learned the Corps doesn't love parades as much as those watching them. When I returned to head Plans and Training on the Commandant's staff, the parade became a logistical problem. Now I was watching the parade critically."

Bob Nulsen was hardly a parade ground soldier. His military career included many real world challenges, as a young lieutenant in Trieste, the hottest spot in the Cold War; as a combat officer in Vietnam, advising Vietnamese Rangers and heading a U.S.

infantry battalion; as a brigade commander with the 82nd Airborne Division. The rows of ribbons on his chest filled out along the way.

"Coming back for our 50th reunion, I see my class moving towards the front of the Long Gray Line," says Nulsen. "We're retired and a lot more open with each other. No one is trying to get up the ladder any further; we've accomplished most of our goals. When they played the West Point March my back stiffened a little bit. There is the cadet part of me that wondered if they are marching as well as we used to march. But then the Tactical Officer in me took over and I said to myself, ' I think they're doing a splendid job.' "

The Association of Graduates roll calls, spanning years and centuries, chronicles both change and constancy. By its Centennial in 1902 there were 4,121 USMA graduates. There are now more than 60,000. Of the 16,000 who have gone on to the final roll call, more than half are buried in the West Point Cemetery. West Point's entering Class of 2006 numbered 1197, 198 of whom are women, 75 African-Americans, 81 Asian and Pacific Islanders, 79 Hispanics and 10 Native Americans.

When President Theodore Roosevelt addressed the 53 white male graduates of West Point's Centennial Class in 1902 he observed, "No other educational institution has contributed so many names as West Point to the honor roll of the nation's greatest citizens."

After General Sherman Hasbrouck headed the Long Gray Line welcoming the Bicentennial Class of 2002, he was asked how things had changed since his graduation in 1920. His response: "They haven't. We all take the same oath."

Ulysses S. Grant, 1843 – Robert E. Lee, 1829
Both answered a call to duty, Grant to head the
Union Army, Lee to lead the Army of Virginia.

George Goethals, 1880 – Leslie Groves, 1918
Leading engineers of the 20th Century: Goethals
Built the Panama Canal, Groves, the atomic
bomb.

Omar Bradley, 1915 – Dwight Eisenhower, 1915
Just 2 of the 59 generals from "The Class The
Stars Fell On" who led American forces to victory
in WW II.

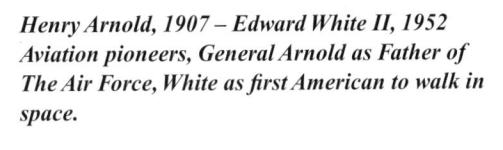

Douglas MacArthur, 1903 –
Maxwell Taylor, 1922
Served as Superintendents of West Point in
mid-career, then went on to become U.S. Army
Chiefs of Staff.

John Pershing, 1882 –
Norman Schwarzkopf, 1956
As majors, taught tactics and engineering at
USMA. As Generals, led victorious forces in WWI
and Desert Storm.

Henry Arnold, 1907 – Edward White II, 1952
Aviation pioneers, General Arnold as Father of
The Air Force, White as first American to walk in
space.

A Gallery of Graduates: A Roll Call of Greatness

Fidel Ramos, 1950 – Jose Maria Figueres, 1979
Philippines President Ramos & Costa Rican
President Figueres studied at USMA as Foreign
Exchange Cadets.

American history will confirm that when duty has called on West Pointers, they have responded with a well-prepared reply. These sixteen graduates, portrayed two by two at various moments in their careers, affirm an insight offered in a lecture to West Point engineers by historian David McCullough.

"You can't slink away from what life lays in your path," said McCullough. He was speaking of Colonel George Goethals' sudden promotion to overall chief of the Panama Canal Project when his predecessor, intimidated by the task, simply left the jungles of Panama. Goethals stood fast and successfully completed one of engineering's most challenging tasks, employing 30,000 people and the largest construction budget of its time.

This gallery is but a hint that, should you take on the mission of learning about these West Pointers and their colleagues, your biographical research will be richly rewarded. Most on these pages had long careers characterized by challenge and growth.

Lt. Richard T. Shea Jr. defended Korea's Pork Chop Hill with heroism "above and beyond the call of duty." Lt. Alexander R. Nininger Jr.'s valor was offered up at the beginning of World War II. A comrade in arms in the Philippines consoled the Nininger family: "… His attitude struck me as a soldier who at last was doing the job he had been trained to do. Men of Company K counted 20 Japanese killed by his grenades. Three Japanese charged towards him with bayonets. He killed all three of them. A counter-attack was made which restored our original line, and made possible the prolongation of the Bataan campaign by months. It is my honest opinion that had not this counterattack been made successfully (based on Nininger's scouting), the entire Bataan campaign would have ended in January instead of three months later. Those three months, I believe, saved Australia and enabled us to end the war many months before it otherwise would have. In my own mind, your son will always be a shining example of what an officer and man should be. He was the most fearless and most courageous officer or soldier I have ever seen."

Alexander Nininger, Jr., 1941 –
Richard Shea, Jr., 1952
Medal of Honor recipients, their valorous deaths
exemplify West Point's "Duty, Honor, Country."

The West Point Cemetery

Many West Point graduates choose to be buried at the Army post where their careers began. As veterans, they are entitled to burial in a government cemetery. As alumni, they take comfort that, at the final roll call, they and their families will be reunited at West Point.

Colonel Sylvanus Thayer, Class of 1808, spiritually heads up the Long Gray Line interred at West Point. Cadets who graduated during his superintendency, 1817-1833, not only made strong contributions to our national defense and prosperity, but also helped found many early American engineering schools. Visitors will find the free pamphlet "A Walking Tour of the West Point Cemetery," at the Visitors Center desk or inside the Old Cadet Chapel, a Greek Revival classic.

Markers range from simple marble headstones to elaborate Victorian mausoleums; the oldest is dated 1782. Visitors will stroll past the graves of Major General George Custer, Civil War Cavalryman and ill-fated Indian fighter, as well as Major General George Goethals, the builder of the Panama Canal. The first American to walk in space, Colonel Edward White II, is buried at West Point along with a host of Lieutenants, Captains, Majors and Colonels who died in combat in distant places but were buried at West Point with full honors.

As one old grad colonel observed, "West Point is home. My wife and I will be buried here. Went to high school here while my father was on the faculty; he and my mother are buried here. I served two tours of duty in Vietnam and three tours of duty at West Point, so my kids were raised here too. There's a whole row of my '64 classmates in there – the Vietnam era. I also see the names of colonels I knew – the backbone of the Army. They had thousands of men and women in their brigade commands and were responsible for millions of dollars of equipment. Awesome responsibility – they paid their dues."

In 1910, as the Old Cadet Chapel was closed – later to be moved stone by stone to its place in the West Point Cemetery – the Cadet Choir offered up a new song. Its words still evoke the cadets' bond with the Long Gray Line preceding them in service to the nation.

America's college class ring tradition began at West Point in 1835.

The Corps! The Corps! The Corps!

The Corps, bareheaded, salute it, With eyes up, thanking our God ✲
That we of the Corps are treading where they of the Corps have trod✲
They are here in ghostly assemblage, the men of the Corps long dead ✲
And our hearts are standing attention while we wait for their passing tread. ✲

We sons of today, we salute you. You, sons of an earlier day; ✲
We follow, close order, behind you, where you have pointed the way; ✲
The Long Gray Line of us stretches Thro' the years of a century told, ✲
And the last man feels to his marrow the grip of your far off hold. ✲

Grip hands with us now though we see not, grip hands with us, strengthen our hearts ✲ As the long line stiffens and straightens with the thrill that your presence imparts. ✲ Grip hands tho' it be from the shadows while we swear, as you did of yore. ✲ Or living, or dying, to honor ✲

✲ The Corps, and the Corps, and the Corps. ✲

The West Point Museum:
Gateway to History

The words on the wall of the entryway say it all. "First opened to the public in 1854, the West Point Museum now holds the largest diversified collection of military arms, flags, uniforms, accouterments, paintings and portraiture in the Western Hemisphere." With 55,000 objects, including 7,700 weapons, who would argue about such a claim?

A first rate curatorial staff, the USMA Department of History and the Academy historian have combined forces to create a very unique museum experience. Keep two important facts in mind when visiting. The museum has always functioned as a component of West Point's courses in military history. It has also been a prime depository for valuable military items that have come into the possession of the United States government.

A visitor first questions the guard. "Which way do we start? Does it make a difference?" A helpful response follows. "Yes it does. Start in the West Point Gallery to my right and take this guide to all six galleries with you."

On entering you will quickly gather that you must circulate around the Museum's upstairs galleries from right to left to get their full value. You are now immersed in a continual story-line experience. Don't skip a sign! Consider yourself to be a cadet, on a four-hour *staff ride* through military history. Your instructor's insights are on the wall and the objects that made military history are right in front of your eyes. Or you can adopt a vacationing father's simple advice to his swiftly moving son during a rewarding one-hour visit. "Read some of the signs so you know what you're looking at!"

The West Point Gallery takes its visitors on a chapter-by-chapter trip through time. *West Point and the Revolution: 1775-1783* displays early paintings of the rugged landscape, a powder horn used by local militia and a mortar captured from the British at Stony Point. There is a sword worn daily by Polish engineer Tadeusz

In 1942, General Jonathan Wainwright's sword was taken after the Philippines fell. In 1945, General Yamashita gave up his sword as the Philippines was liberated. After World War II ended with a stroke of General MacArthur's pen, all three objects arrived at the museum's History of Warfare Gallery.

BREECHLOADERS

M en went over to fight battles has seen a war difficult and to use hard much deciding historian to any other premise. breechloading wheeled value and even earlier never as turned use by the 16th century, but they were useful once because of gas leakage in the breech. The reason was the problem of sealing the breech was the blast cartridge close to be ready until the breech when loading, but when the weapon was fired the gas pressure expanded it, forming a tight seal. After the bullet left the barrel, the gas pressure dropped, allowing the cartridge case to contract and be removed easily. Designers soon captured the near perfection of the answer to the 20th century, but it's application had to wait until the mid-19th century when it became possible to produce cartridge cases quickly and cheaply.

In 1870, almost every army in the world had adopted a breech loading rifle. Together with rifling, this improvement enabled soldiers to fight at greater distances, to volley fire, and to fire from any position.

Ferguson Breechloading Flintlock Rifle, c. 1700, Caliber .65

Major Patrick Ferguson of the British 71st Highland Regiment developed this rifle and demonstrated it to a Board of Officers at Woolwich, England, in the spring of 1776. One form of the weapon featured the breech mechanism sufficient to expose the chamber, allowing ball and powder to be loaded into the breech. One of the major advantages to fire an exact per minute while standing and four shots per minute while advancing at a time when most rifles were accurate that the common musket was capable of producing.

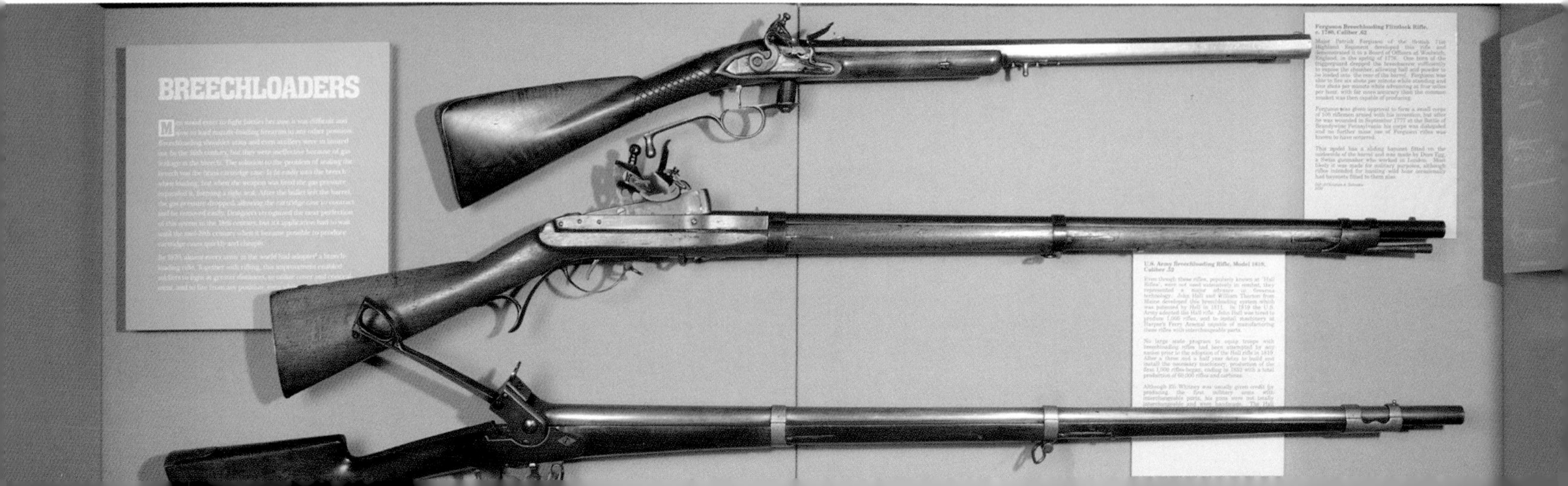

Ferguson was given approval to form a small corps of 100 riflemen armed with his invention, but after he was wounded in September 1777 at the Battle of Brandywine, Pennsylvania, his corps was disbanded and no further issue use of Ferguson rifles was known to have occurred.

This model has a sliding bayonet fitted to the underside of the barrel and was made in Dusn Egg, a Swiss gunmaker who worked in London. Most likely it was made for military purposes, although rifles intended for hunting with bore occasionally had bayonets fitted to them also.

U.S. Army Breechloading Rifle, Model 1819, Caliber .52

Even though these rifles, popularly known as "Hall Rifles," were not used extensively in combat, they represented a major advance in firearms technology. John Hall and William Thornton first patented this breechloading system which was patented by Hall in 1811. In 1819 the U.S. Army adopted the Hall rifle, the first one ever to produce 1,000 rifles, and to detail machinery at Harper's Ferry Armory capable of manufacturing these rifles with interchangeable parts.

So large scale program to equip troops with breechloading rifles had been attempted by any nation prior to the adoption of the Hall rifle in 1819. After a slow start a half year delay to build and install the machinery necessary to manufacture the first 1,000 rifles, ending in 1824 with a total production of 50,000 rifles and carbines.

Although Eli Whitney was usually given credit for producing the first military arms with interchangeable parts, the Hall rifles were the first interchangeable and first to make use of machinery designed expressly for that purpose.

Kosciuszko, and a model of the British Sloop-of-War Vulture that rescued the traitorous General Benedict Arnold.

The First Engineering Academy: 1817-1865 has a well-coordinated presentation of words and objects that speak of the new nation's desire to become technologically independent from Europe. Other periods of history are covered fully with unique displays. Listen as you tour and you will hear fellow visitors speaking Japanese, German, Chinese and Russian. They are respectfully studying how West Point gained its worldwide stature.

Once the West Point Gallery gets you into military history, it would be a good idea to visit the basement galleries where you should proceed from left to right. As you enter the Small Weapons Gallery, you will see a simple stone-age dagger. Concise words describe this meaningful display. "From earliest times, man has fashioned tools and implements. From axes and clubs through the development of light machine guns, the evolution of individual weapons has influenced tactics, organization and strategy, serving to advance technology and act as a catalyst for further development." Advances in weaponry pass in review within 20 display cases labeled "Clubs, Axes, Knives, Swords, Wall Guns, Polearms, Hand Cannon, Match Locks, Wheellocks, Flintlocks, Percussion, Breechloaders, Assault Rifles, Submachine Guns, Light Machine Guns, Pistols."

One woman visitor remarked that her husband had patiently been dragged through art museums for a week. "Now he gets to see the good stuff." His favorite in a sea of mechanical marvels was the Liberator Pistol, a one-time use, single shot model developed by General Motors in 1942. The rationale: "It was believed a partisan could kill an enemy soldier with the pistol and rearm himself with the enemy's weapons."

Logistics: GM said it could supply 2 million per week for $2.00 each. Outcome: only 1 million were ordered. The rest of the story lies downstairs in the Large Weapons Gallery. At the conclusion of a parade of cannons, machine guns and army vehicles, you encounter the ballistic case

The Army of the Potomac still marches up Pennsylvania Avenue in Washington D.C., at least in the America's Wars Gallery.

for the "Fat Boy" atomic bomb dropped at Nagasaki. The history of national defense has always been a tug-of-war between cunning and strength.

Returning upstairs, you now have a better visual vocabulary to view the informative presentations in *the History of Warfare, American Army and American Wars* galleries. Dioramas of great battles in history await your mental war games. Look for the Civil War Surgeon's kit, Napoleon's sword and pistols, German Field Marshall Goering's jewel encrusted baton of office, and a case with eight different helmet styles, representing the allied opposition to World War II's Axis Powers. A lot to see. And, don't forget the Museum gift shop. Its excellent book selection offers take-home for awakened minds.

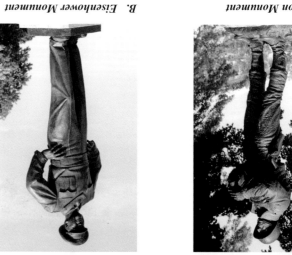

D. *MacArthur Monument*

C. *Washington Monument*

B. *Eisenhower Monument*

A. *Patton Monument*